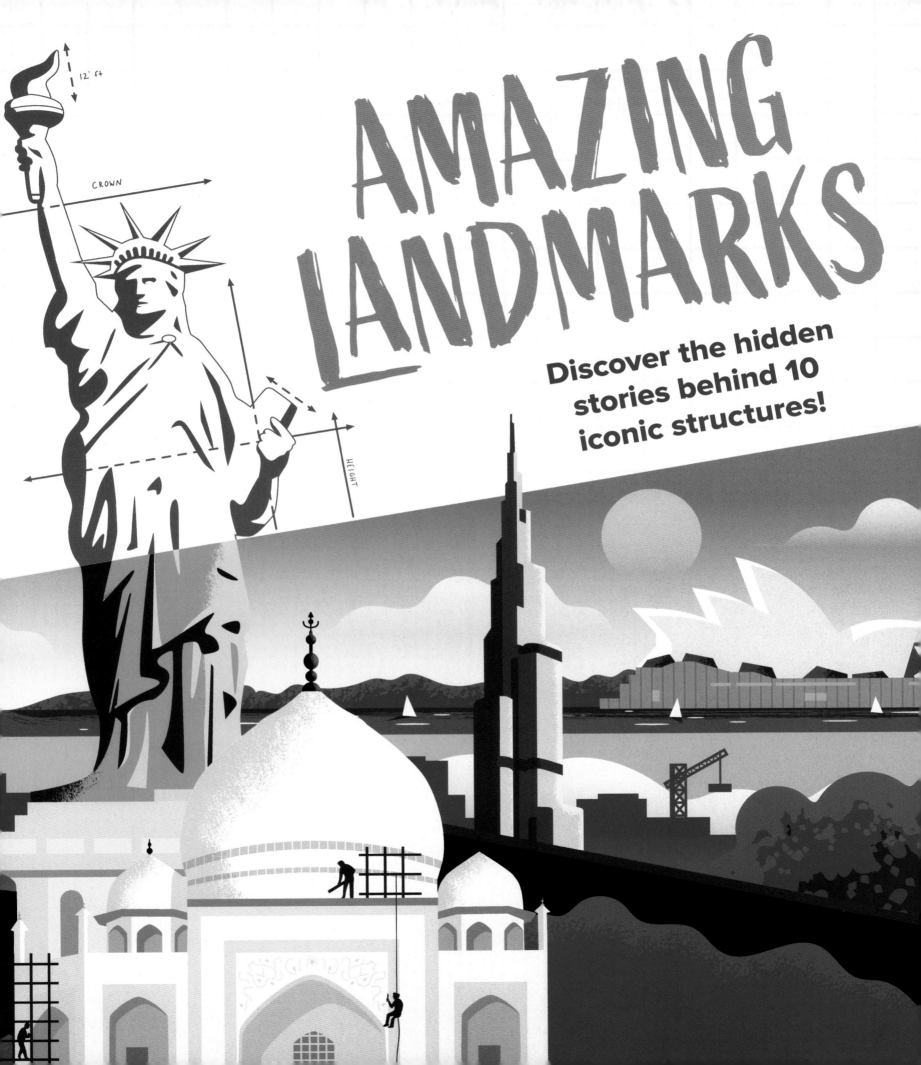

AMAZING LANDMARKS

Discover the hidden stories behind 10 iconic structures!

12' ft

CROWN

HEIGHT

For Jagan, Madhavi, and Arjun,
my builders and dreamers.
—RSR

To my parents, Annemarie and Khalil,
thanks for showing me the world.
—AA

Text copyright © 2022 by Rekha S. Rajan
Art copyright © 2022 by Alex Asfour

Library of Congress Cataloging-in-Publication Data Available

Photos ©: 8: Bettmann/Getty Images; 9: Banepetkovic/Dreamstime; 15: NASA; 19: Dinodia Photos/Alamy Stock Photo; 20 top: The Picture Art Collection/Alamy Stock Photo; 20 bottom: Subhrajyoti Parida/Dreamstime; 23 top: Sisirbanga/Dreamstime; 24: Smithore/Dreamstime; 25 bottom: Samrat35/Dreamstime; 29 top: fotosmania/Getty Images; 29 bottom: The Picture Art Collection/Alamy Stock Photo; 30: ART Collection/Alamy Stock Photo; 31: gianliguori/Getty Images; 34 top: Jon Arnold Images Ltd/Alamy Stock Photo; 34 bottom: CARL DE SOUZA/AFP/Getty Images; 35 top: TomasSereda/Getty Images; 38: Library of Congress; 39: Hi-Story/Alamy Stock Photo; 41: Jef Wodniack/Getty Images; 42 bottom: FPG/Getty Images; 43: Svisio/Getty Images; 44: Library of Congress; 45: Niday Picture Library/Alamy Stock Photo; 48-49: Pictorial Press Ltd/Alamy Stock Photo; 49: Photos.com/Getty Images; 51 right: Interim Archives/Getty Images; 53: Creativemarc/Getty Images; 60 top: Library of Congress; 60 bottom: PeterHermesFurian/Getty Images; 62: Library of Congress; 63: Paulo Costa/Getty Images; 64: Library of Congress; 65 top: Victor Ward/Getty Images; 65 bottom: User10095428_393/Getty Images; 68: diegograndi/Getty Images; 71: Bettmann/Getty Images; 72: Library of Congress; 80 top: Abbus Archive Images/Alamy Stock Photo; 80 bottom: Fairfax Media/Getty Images; 84: JohnCarnemolla/Getty Images; 85 top: Ian Cumming/Axiom Photographic/age fotostock; 85 bottom: Denis Pepin/Dreamstime; 88: Kravka/Dreamstime; 89 top: Stuart Lutz/Gado/Getty Images; 89 bottom: Michelle McDonald/Getty Images; 90: vPaulTech LLC/Getty Images; 91: elinedesignservices/Getty Images; 93 bottom: Bettmann/Getty Images; 93 top: Library of Congress; 95: John McDonnell/The Washington Post/Getty Images; 101 left: At the Top, Burj Khalifa & Emaar Entertainment; 103 top: Ashestosky/Dreamstime; 103 bottom: Igor Sorokin/Alamy Stock Vector. All other photos © Shutterstock.com.

ISBN 978-1-338-65249-9

10 9 8 7 6 5 4 3 2 1   22 23 24 25 26

Printed in China   62

First edition, March 2022
Cover design by Brian LaRossa
Interior design by Maria Lilja

Written by **Rekha S. Rajan**   Illustrated by **Alex Asfour**

AMAZING LANDMARKS

SCHOLASTIC PRESS ▲ **NEW YORK**

TABLE OF CONTENTS

INTRODUCTION

If you were asked to connect two big cities across a large body of water,

▶ *What materials would you use?*

If you were asked to make the world's tallest building,

▶ *How much money would you need?*

If you were asked to design a statue,

▶ *Who would be on your team?*

▶ *What would you name it?*

And . . .

▶ *Could you BUILD IT?*

The tallest, biggest, longest, widest, and most famous landmarks and structures in the world took years to build. Each landmark needed a design, budget, materials, color choices, and a team that would make very important decisions. The teams also had to battle the weather, including strong winds, icy hail, or burning heat; raise a fortune; and overcome the challenges that come with creating a unique design.

As you read:

Identify the materials and budget.

Analyze the weather and environment.

Choose what role you would play on the team.

Decide if YOU could BUILD IT!

The Great Wall of China

China, 220 CE

THE PROBLEM!

The fifth century BCE was a peaceful time in China. The Spring and Autumn period of the Zhou dynasty was an era of teaching and learning. The philosopher Confucius spoke about how people should always be kind and fair, even in battle!

The lands were divided by the feudal system. The kingdom consisted of fiefs (pieces of land) that were ruled by the Zhou king and his relatives.

IT'S HISTORY!
This is the same system that was used a thousand years later during the Middle Ages in Europe!

Soon, these rulers stopped supporting the king. They wanted more power for themselves and began to battle one another.

Bronze workers were very busy making protective armor and shields.

▶ *Would you rather design and build the armor or wear it and fight?*

Battles began to take place nearly every day as warriors from one state invaded another. Still, the soldiers fought with honor! They followed rules to make sure that everyone had a fair chance to win. But as the battles continued for many years, the state leaders grew worried.

State leaders had a BIG problem!

What could they build to stop the battles and invasions?

GREEK ARMOR FROM THE BRONZE AGE.

THE SOLUTION!

Walls!

Each state leader decided to build a small wall to protect themselves and their people from the neighboring states.

By 260 BCE, the smaller fiefs were all ruled by seven large warring states: Qin, Chu, Zhao, Wei, Han, Yan, and Qi.

But some people were *still* unhappy! Shang Yang, a leader from the Wei state, went to the neighboring Qin state to talk to their leader. He said he was tired of following the rules! He left the Wei state behind and helped the Qin state build their military and economy.

Charge!

After one long, tiring battle, the Qin state took over all the others and became the strongest state of all.

Qin Shi Huang, the ruler of the newly formed Qin dynasty, unified China and became the leader of all the states. This meant he was not just a king, but an emperor! He saw how important the walls were for safety and protection. A tribe of the Mongol people known as the Xiongnu lived north of China and kept trying to invade the now-peaceful country. What could Qin Shi Huang do?

Then he had an idea.

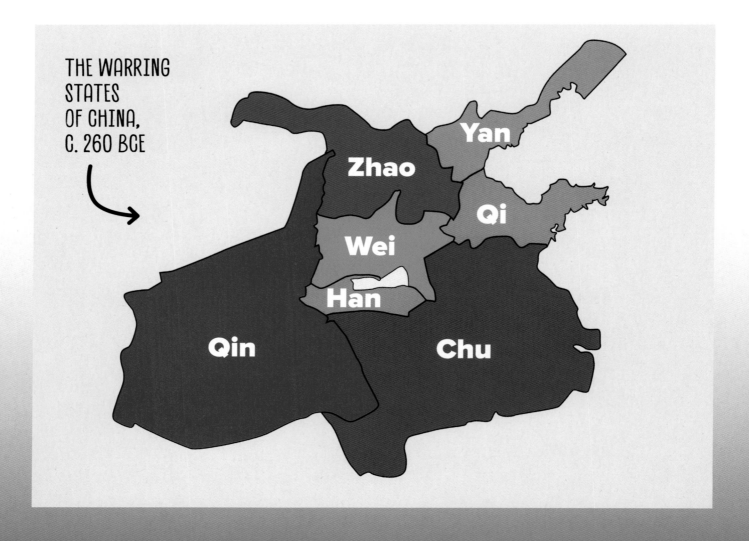

THE WARRING STATES OF CHINA, C. 260 BCE

Zhao

Yan

Qi

Wei

Han

Qin

Chu

He could connect all the smaller walls throughout the country and build one big, strong wall that would keep China's northern border safe from invasion!

THE TEAM!

Qin Shi Huang ordered over one million warriors and prisoners to build the wall. Many of the warriors had to leave their families and children behind. Some of them never returned home.

BUDGET IT!

As the emperor of China, Qin Shi Huang decided to use the money he collected through taxes to pay for the construction of the wall.

MATH FACT

During this time, coins were still a new invention, and many people didn't use them for money yet! So taxes included giving grain or other goods to the government.

DESIGN IT!

The wall needed to have a very specific design. It had to wind through twisty mountains and over rough terrain. The emperor also wanted watchtowers so warriors could keep a lookout in case invaders were coming!

The wall had to protect very important trade routes. This included pathways that went into the large, hot Gobi Desert.

Which of these other landmarks was important for trade?

A. The Taj Mahal

B. The Panama Canal

C. The Eiffel Tower

D. Big Ben

If you picked *B*, you're right! The Panama Canal helped *decrease* the time needed to trade by ship, while the Great Wall helped to *increase* the safety of people traveling on trade routes.

IT'S HISTORY!

This route was later named the "Silk Road" because people living in Europe loved to trade for the silk that came from China and other Asian countries. Other items that were traded on these routes include gold, ivory, tea, and plants.

NAME IT!

Although it is called the Great Wall of China, the name of the wall is actually *Wànlǐ Chángchéng*, which means "Ten Thousand Li Long Wall." One li was equal to about 1,640 feet.

GOBI DESERT

BUILD IT!

It was time to begin building!

Workers had to lift big stones and rocks on their backs and carry the loads from the quarries to the base of the wall. The rocks were very heavy! Sometimes the workers attached ropes to a bar and hung the rocks from the rope. Then they put the bar on their shoulders to transport the materials. This method was later used in other countries to make stretchers and carry patients who were sick.

Look out!

Rocks tumbled to the ground! The sides of the mountain were steep! Workers slipped and fell. Many got hurt trying to lift and place the heavy stones. If there were any gaps in the wall, the holes were filled with rocks or used as a place to bury those who died.

After the Qin dynasty ended, several other dynasties came and went. Workers continued building sections of the wall for hundreds of years. As the smaller walls were connected, soldiers marched through the watchtowers and took their positions! They communicated with one another using smoke signals and fires.

LITTER IN SHANGHAI, C. 1860

Oh no!

While the walls were still being built, China was invaded by Emperor Genghis Khan and his Mongol warriors!

People started to get worried. *Would the wall really protect them from invasion?*

FINISHING TOUCHES!

Construction of the wall slowed down. It took almost one hundred years, but the Mongol Empire was finally defeated and sent out of China. By then, the Ming dynasty had formed and a new emperor took charge.

The Ming leaders knew they had to make changes to the wall to make it more effective. The workers now used stronger materials, like limestone and granite. Donkeys and horses were brought in to help carry the heavy rocks and stones and finish the wall.

EMPEROR GENGHIS KHAN OF THE MONGOL EMPIRE

ENGINEERING EXTRA

Many people believe that the wall can be seen from space! Can you find it?

Here it is again, with arrows to help you see sections of the wall! This picture was taken in 2004 by astronaut Leroy Chiao from a low orbit around Earth. He used a digital camera with a 180 mm lens.

UNVEIL IT!

In 1878, the leaders of China decided to stop building the wall. The weapons that people used in battle had changed. There was no reason to continue building, and there was no special ceremony to celebrate finishing the wall. Instead, the Great Wall of China stood as a symbol of the country's strength.

When it was finished, the wall:

- Was the longest wall in the world—all of its sections added together equal 13,173 miles.
- Had taken the longest amount of time to build of any landmark, at over two thousand years.

In 1987, the United Nations Educational, Scientific and Cultural Organization (UNESCO) designated the Great Wall a World Heritage site. Although the complete total is unknown, it is estimated that, translated into today's money, the Great Wall of China cost 90 billion dollars to build.

Over time, around 30 percent of the wall became damaged from corrosion. The government of China has put many laws in place to protect the wall, including some that save money for its *restoration*. When you visit, don't take a piece of the wall as a souvenir! It is a crime.

Even though the states of China battled one another for power, faced threats of invaders, and took over two thousands years, they were finally able to **BUILD IT!**

🔍 **DEFINE IT**

Restoration is the process of fixing and updating a structure, building, or piece of art.

MATH FACT

It would take almost two years to walk the entire stretch of the wall! *If you started walking today, how old would you be when you got to the end?*

CITY FACT

The section in Badaling, by Beijing, is the most restored and most visited part of the wall.

The Taj Mahal

Agra, India, 1653

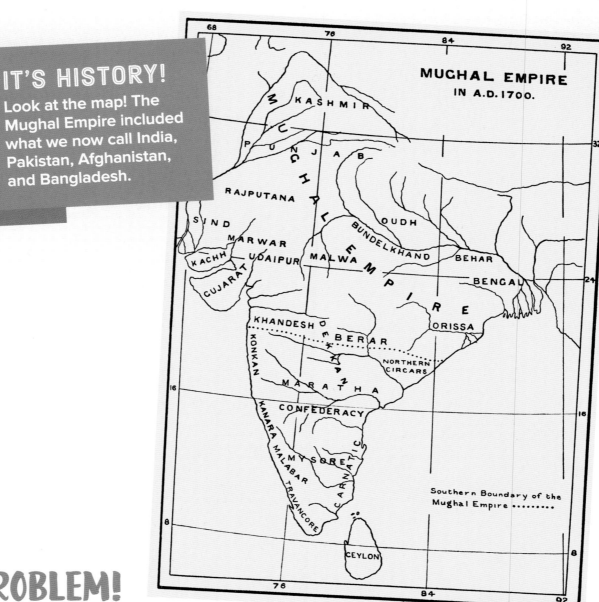

THE PROBLEM!

Ah, true love!

In 1612, Shah Jahan (also known as Prince Khurram) married Arjumand Banu Begum. He nicknamed her "Mumtaz Mahal." In the Persian language, her name meant "the beautiful one of the palace." It was love at first sight!

Shah Jahan and Mumtaz Mahal were both from royal families. She was a princess, and he was the son of an emperor. In 1628, they became the emperor and empress of the Mughal Empire! This was one of the longest dynasties in history; it stretched from the sixteenth to the nineteenth century.

Mumtaz Mahal and Shah Jahan had thirteen children. They traveled everywhere together. Sometimes they even battled against armies while riding horses! *CHARGE!*

But on one journey, Mumtaz Mahal died while giving birth to their fourteenth child. Shah Jahan was heartbroken. How could he rule without her?

Shah Jahan had a BIG problem!

What could he do to show the entire world how much he loved and missed his wife?

PEACOCK THRONE

DESIGN DETAIL

Look closely! The minarets lean slightly outward. In case of an earthquake, Shah Jahan did not want the towers to crush the center!

THE SOLUTION!

Shah Jahan loved building! He wanted to build beautiful structures everywhere. He even built himself a "Peacock Throne" made of silver, gold, and decorative peacocks covered in diamonds and rubies. He decided to build a monument for his wife. He wanted it to be the biggest, most beautiful building in the Mughal Empire. It was his symbol of eternal love for the world to admire!

▶ *If you could build yourself a throne, what would you design?*

THE TEAM!

As emperor, he invited famous artists to help, including:

- An *architect* to design the monument and surrounding land.
- A *designer* to add details through art and jewels.
- A *sculptor* to shape the towers and the curves of the domes.
- A *calligrapher* to draw beautiful words and lines.

BUDGET IT!

Shah Jahan had a lot of money, both from his family and from his position as emperor. He spent 35 million rupees. That would be almost one billion dollars today!

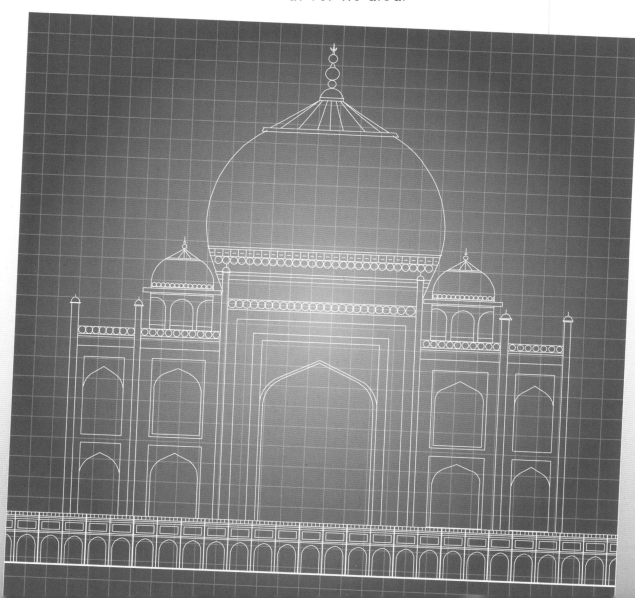

DESIGN IT!

Ustad Ahmad Lahori was asked to design a spectacular monument that would be a mausoleum, or aboveground resting place, for Mumtaz Mahal's body. He drew a center building with a dome that would be 240 feet tall, then added four minarets on the perimeter. These small towers were *perpendicular* to the floor plan of the center building. Each minaret would stand 130 feet tall.

 DEFINE IT

Perpendicular means the towers form a 90-degree angle at their base!

There would be a main entrance, a garden, a mosque, a *jawāb* (in Arabic, this means an "answer" or "reflection" of the mosque), and the mausoleum. Ustad Ahmad Lahori also drew a lavish garden at the entrance. The tomb inside the mausoleum where Mumtaz Mahal would be laid was at the garden level. The floor plan was perfectly *symmetrical* no matter how you looked at it: vertically, horizontally, or diagonally.

DEFINE IT

Symmetrical means it is exactly the same on both sides.

Mumtaz Mahal would lie in the center and Shah Jahan would be next to her after he died.

NAME IT!

The name "Taj Mahal" is Persian for "crown palace."

▶ *If you could name a building after someone you love, what would you name it?*

BUILD IT!

Now it was time to find the right place to build the palace! As emperor, Shah Jahan wanted to see the monument from his position in Agra Fort.

Where could he build?

The river!

The Yamuna River was a very important body of water for both the Islamic and Hindu religions. People believed the water was pure and had healing powers. It still flows today.

The construction team got to work! Over twenty thousand people helped to dig out the land. First, the sandy bank of the river had to be set. Builders dug deep wells and then covered them with wood. Next, they added iron and rubble as a foundation.

Shah Jahan wanted the purest white marble to frame the monument. He went to the Makrana mines in Rajasthan, India, and mined a unique marble called *sang-i-rukham*.

▶ *How do you think the marble feels? Smooth? Rough? Sticky?*

Oh no!

The marble was too heavy for people to carry. The builders needed to find a way to transport the marble to the building site. There were no cars, trucks, or planes! What could they use?

MAKRANA MARBLE
FROM THE TAJ MAHAL

MAKRANA
MARBLE
QUARRY

IT'S HISTORY!

In 2019, Makrana marble was designated a Global Heritage Stone Resource because of its historical and cultural value. It was also used in the Victoria Memorial in Kolkata, India, which was built for Queen Victoria of the United Kingdom.

23

Elephants!

Over one thousand elephants were used to transport the materials. It looked like a parade!

The Taj Mahal is not made entirely of marble. The design team used red sandstone for the base. This was to make sure the monument stood strong before the marble was placed on the frame. The large center dome is shaped like an onion and sits on a base shaped like a drum.

Builders also added hundreds of fragrant trees and foliage to the garden as soon as construction started. This was so the trees would have time to grow!

DESIGN DETAIL

Did you know that the Taj Mahal changes colors throughout the day? The sun reflects off the marble in different ways. In the morning, it looks pink; during the afternoon, it looks white; and in the evening, it shines like gold!

IT'S HISTORY!

When the British ruled over India in the nineteenth century, they changed the gardens. They cut down roses, foliage, and fruit trees to make the grounds look more open.

Builders worked for seventeen years to complete the terrace, mausoleum, and minarets. During this time, Shah Jahan gathered over twenty-eight different types of gemstones to decorate the Taj Mahal. These included jade from China, turquoise from Tibet, lapis lazuli from Afghanistan, and jasper from Punjab. Look at all the different colored stones! Some of these are also birthstones.

▶ *What is your birthstone? Is it on the Taj Mahal?*

FINISHING TOUCHES!

Calligraphers painted beautiful images on the walls. According to Islamic tradition, artists were not allowed to draw people or animals. Instead, there are many floral details that were inspired by Italian art. This process of carving stone with gems is called *pietra dura,* an art form that originated during the Renaissance in Europe!

▶ *Can you name a famous artist from the Renaissance?*

DESIGN DETAIL
The style is called Indo-Islamic—that means it includes traditional Hindu art and Islamic art. It's a mix of two religions!

UNVEIL IT!

The Taj Mahal was finished in 1653. The palace:

- Took 22 years to build.
- Covered 42 acres of land.

Over 7 million people visit the Taj Mahal every year. In 1983, it was designated a UNESCO World Heritage site, which means it is an important global monument because of how it looks and what it represents. It is also one of the New Seven Wonders of the World!

Even though the Taj Mahal is a mausoleum, it is also a palace and has a guesthouse with 120 rooms. In 2019, the government of India began allowing visitors to spend the night.

▶ *Would you want to spend the night in the Taj Mahal?*

Shah Jahan had to overcome many challenges, including finding the perfect place to build, transporting heavy marble, and making sure he showed the whole world how much he loved (and missed) his wife. But after all the hard work, he and his team were able to **BUILD IT!**

TOURISM FACT

Don't visit on a Friday! The Taj Mahal is closed for prayers in the mosque.

SCIENCE SAFETY

Cough, cough! The city of Agra is covered in smog! Dust and dirt particles fill the air. Is the Taj Mahal safe from corrosion?

In 2019, the government of India built a special air purifier to try to keep the air around the monument clean. Only electric cars can drive by, and the air above it is a no-fly zone!

Big Ben

London, England, 1859

THE PROBLEM!

In 1834, London was the biggest city in the world! It was a trade center and had the largest port in Europe for ferries and ships to dock.

It was an exciting time. People were finding new ways to travel around the city. One invention was the hansom cab. It was a carriage that had two wheels and was pulled by a horse!

▶ *Would you rather take a ride in the hansom cab or steer the horse?*

But this was also the beginning of the Victorian era, and over half the city was poor. Some families did not have enough food. Others ate only bread and butter every day. Charles Dickens was an author living in London at this time. He wrote about these struggles in his famous stories, such as *Oliver Twist* and *A Christmas Carol*.

On October 16, 1834, a terrible fire burned the Palace of Westminster! This was where Parliament and the other leaders of the British government worked.

BOOM! The wooden panels burst as the fire came up from stoves under the floor. The fire spread quickly as everyone ran out to escape.

People stood on boats in the River Thames watching the blaze cover the sky.

When the fire finally stopped and the building crumbled to the ground, people were relieved that the city was still safe. But . . .

London had a BIG problem!

Where would the country's leaders work now?

A HANSOM CAB

29

THE SOLUTION!

A new structure!

The British leaders knew they needed to find a place for the Houses of Parliament, which included the House of Lords and the House of Commons. This time, they wanted to add a tower and a clock! But who would design it?

THE TEAM!

The year was now 1835, and the leaders needed to find:

- An *architect* to draw and build the structure.
- A *designer* to decorate the interior and the clock tower.
- *Geologists* to find the best stone for the structure.

So, they held . . .

A contest!

Architects from all over London sent in their ideas. The winner was . . .

Sir Charles Barry! He was already a very famous British architect. Barry then asked his friend Augustus Pugin to design the clock tower. Barry and Pugin worked together to draw the new structure. They decided the clock tower should stand on the north side of the palace and have four equal-size clock faces that would light up at night!

SIR CHARLES BARRY

BUDGET IT!

Barry was given 700,000 pounds to build the palace. That would be almost 30 million dollars today! He paid Pugin 400 pounds to add Gothic elements to the design. He also said he could build the structure in just six years.

Now it was time to design!

DESIGN IT!

Barry had to create a design that would help the members of Parliament. He drew the Queen's throne, the Lords Chamber, and the Commons Chamber in one straight line so they were linked together! He added paneling and turrets that would be built high above the building.

Barry also asked for help from Benjamin Lewis Vulliamy—the Queen's official clockmaker. Vulliamy drew a design for the clock, but other clockmakers living in London wanted a chance, too! So, the leaders held . . .

WESTMINSTER PALACE TODAY

Another contest!

The judge was Sir George Airy, the Queen's astronomy expert. He asked if anyone could build a clock that would show the first stroke of each hour *accurately* on all four sides. The clock tower would also have a bell inside that would ring loudly throughout the day!

Who could build it?

Many people entered the contest, but it was difficult to design such a big clock. After seven years, an experienced clockmaker named Edward John Dent was finally announced as the winner.

DEFINE IT

Accurate means to be exact or correct in every detail.

NAME IT!

Since the Palace of Westminster was being rebuilt, the city of London called the tower the Great Westminster Clock Tower. No one really knows where the name Big Ben came from, but it is actually the name of the biggest bell in the tower—not the clock!

IT'S HISTORY!

In 2012, the House of Commons voted and renamed the tower the Elizabeth Tower in honor of Queen Elizabeth II.

BUILD IT!

Barry and two geologists on his team toured rock quarries all around England. They wanted to find the best limestone for the structure. They chose limestone from Anston Quarry because it was inexpensive and easy to carve.

First, the builders laid the limestone bricks to form the base. Then they added concrete to act as a raft for the clock tower. The frame of the tower was built with cast iron and copper. The builders used 91,000 cubic feet of brick.

The builders worked on the inside and outside of the clock. They had to be careful while standing on the scaffolding. One slip, and they might fall into the River Thames!

Soon, the clock face was ready to be pushed in. *CLICK!* The glass was set. It protected the large hands that would tell the time. The hands of the clock were very big! The little hand was nine feet long, and the big hand was fourteen feet long! That is as tall as a baby and mother giraffe.

IT'S HISTORY!
During World War II, the clock face was kept dark at night so that enemy aircraft would have a hard time finding and attacking it.

DESIGN DETAIL
Each number on the dial is two feet tall. *How tall are you compared to the clock numbers?*

The gigantic bell was tested before it was put into the clock tower. *CRACK!* The bell broke and would not ring. The builders made a new bell and lifted it up into the tower. But then—*CRACK!* The new bell broke, too! This time, they figured out a way to fix it without replacing the whole thing.

SCIENCE SAFETY

Don't stand too close. The sound from Big Ben measures 118 decibels. That is so loud it could hurt your ears. You would also feel the vibrations shake your entire body!

CITY FACT

When Big Ben was constructed, the city of London was much smaller than it is today. When it first rang, it could be heard over nine miles away!

ENGINEERING EXTRA

Did you know that there are actually five bells inside the clock tower? Big Ben is the largest and weighs almost 15 tons. That is as heavy as five elephants!

FINISHING TOUCHES!

Next, the gears were added inside the clock tower. Like most clocks, it has three sets, or "trains," of gears:

- The *going train* rotates the hands.
- The *chiming train* makes the clock chime every 15 minutes.
- The *striking train* makes Big Ben chime every hour.

The engineers added heavy weights to the cables inside the clock. As gravity pulls the weights down toward the ground, they turn the cables, which rotates the trains.

▶ *Which train of gears would you want to be in charge of, and why?*

Finally, Latin words were inscribed under each clock face. They say: "*Domine Salvam fac Reginam nostram Victoriam primam*," which means "Lord, keep our Queen Victoria safe."

DESIGN DETAIL

The tower was built in the Gothic style of architecture, with pointed archways and tall spires. This is just like the cathedral of Notre-Dame in Paris, France.

IT'S HISTORY!

There is another famous bell halfway across the world. Look at the Liberty Bell in Philadelphia, Pennsylvania, in the United States. *How are the bells the same? How are they different?*

UNVEIL IT!

Look at Big Ben! When it was finished, it was:

- The tallest clock tower in the world, at 315 feet.
- The biggest bell in the world, with a diameter of 9 feet.

It took over thirty years to rebuild the Palace of Westminster and cost over 2 million pounds. That was double the original budget!

On July 11, 1859, the bell rang for the first time! Everyone cheered.

When you visit, watch where you step. There is a lot of pigeon poop scattered around the tower. Yuck!

Today, the Makkah Royal Clock Tower in Saudi Arabia has the biggest clock face in the world. But Big Ben still stands as the most recognized and photographed clock tower and has kept time in London for over 160 years!

Even though the original Palace of Westminster burned down and Sir Charles Barry had to find the right designers, engineers, and clockmakers, he overcame these challenges and was able to **BUILD IT!**

IT'S HISTORY!
On May 31, 2009, Big Ben turned 150 years old! The city of London had a big celebration. Hooray!

ENGINEERING EXTRA
On August 21, 2017, the clock went silent for five years for repairs.

TOURISM FACT

You can't go on a tour of Big Ben unless you are a resident of the United Kingdom. You also have to be over eleven years old and able to climb 334 steps!

The Statue of Liberty

New York City, United States, 1886

THE PROBLEM!

Best friends forever!

The United States and France were very good friends. In 1783, France helped America beat Britain to win the American Revolution. Then, in 1865, slavery was abolished in the United States and the American Civil War came to an end. France wanted to give the United States something special to celebrate. This gift would be a symbol of friendship and alliance.

But France had a BIG problem!

What gift could they give?

THE SOLUTION!

Édouard René de Laboulaye, president of the French Anti-Slavery Society, was a political leader with great ideas. He thought France could give . . .

A statue!

He said that a statue would be a great monument and symbol of independence. A sculptor named Frédéric-Auguste Bartholdi heard of this idea and began to sketch designs. De Laboulaye loved them!

THE TEAM!

Bartholdi needed a great team to help build his sculpture. He was the lead designer, but he also needed:

- An *engineer* to help build the sculpture and choose the right materials.
- A *financier* to pay for the statue to be built and shipped to the United States.
- *Builders* to hammer the materials into the perfect shape.

FRENCH SCULPTOR
FRÉDÉRIC-AUGUSTE BARTHOLDI

BUDGET IT!

Bartholdi was in luck. France agreed that the sculpture would be a great gift of friendship and celebration. He received 2,250,000 francs from the government. That would be over 10 million dollars today!

De Laboulaye and Bartholdi signed a letter of introduction to say who they were and what they wanted to do. Bartholdi took the letter and went off to visit the United States to share the good news!

DESIGN IT!

First stop, Bedloe's Island, New York City!

Bartholdi thought it was the perfect spot for the statue. He wanted the statue to represent freedom and peace. During this time, artists traditionally *personified* America as a Roman goddess, who was called Columbia, meaning the goddess of liberty. Bartholdi decided the sculpture should be in her image. This style is called "neoclassicism," since the design is chiefly inspired by ancient art.

 **DEFINE IT**

To *personify* means "to give humanlike qualities to something nonhuman." It's like saying, "The wind howled at night."

CITY FACT

Bedloe's Island was later named Liberty Island, and the Statue of Liberty National Monument also includes the famous Ellis Island!

IT'S HISTORY!

Ancient Romans believed in the goddess Libertas, who was another form of the goddess of liberty.

Bartholdi used his mom as a model! He drew her wearing a long, draping gown and cloak and holding a torch in her right hand. In her left hand, he wanted her to hold a tablet that read:

July IV MDCCLXXVI

July 4, 1776. Independence Day!

▶ *What would you write on her tablet, and why?*

He also added chains and a broken shackle by her feet to represent the end of slavery in the US.

NAME IT!

Picking a name was easy. Since she carries a torch and represents Libertas—the Roman goddess of freedom—the design team titled the sculpture . . .

Liberty enlightening the world!

But most often, people call her the Statue of Liberty for short, or Lady Liberty.

IT'S HISTORY!
Bartholdi designed a massive sculpture called the Lion of Belfort that still stands in France. *ROAR!*

BUILD IT!

Bartholdi asked his friend Eugène Viollet-le-Duc to be the head engineer. Viollet-le-Duc decided that the skin of the statue should be made of large copper sheets. These would be heated up and then hit with hammers. It was a technique called *repoussé.* This is the same way that King Tut's burial mask was made in ancient Egypt.

BAM! Builders needed over 300 different types of hammers to get the copper into the right shape!

The copper is the same as what you can find on a penny. The design team also put seven spikes on the crown—one for each of the seven continents.

▶ *How many spikes would you put on the crown, and why?*

KING TUT'S BURIAL MASK

CITY FACT
The statue's head was originally an exhibit at the Paris World's Fair in 1878. People climbed inside and walked up to her crown! The Eiffel Tower was unveiled at the next Paris World's Fair, in 1889.

The head and right arm were finished!

There was a lot left to build. But Viollet-le-Duc became very sick and died before the statue could be completed. Bartholdi needed to find a new engineer—quickly! Who could help?

Gustave Eiffel said he could design the inside of the statue. Eiffel wanted the sculpture to be hollow and open. He made an iron skeleton that could bend and move in the gusty winds without collapsing! He also added a staircase that twisted in the shape of a double helix. That is the same shape as the DNA molecules in our bodies.

Now visitors would be able to climb all the way to the crown and back down!

DNA MOLECULES

ENGINEERING EXTRA
Can you guess what other famous structure Gustave Eiffel built?

ENGINEERING EXTRA
The statue started to turn green in 1900. This was because *patina*, a thin layer of acid, began to form on the statue and spread all over! Engineers first thought it was corrosion, but then realized the patina actually protected the outer layer of copper and kept it!

FINISHING TOUCHES!

The pieces were complete. It was time to ship it to New York City to be assembled!

Oh no!

The leaders of the United States didn't have enough money to pay for the final piece of the statue.

The base!

They needed 100,000 dollars to finish the pedestal and pay for shipping costs. That would be almost 5 million dollars today! How would they get the money to finish the statue and assemble it in New York City?

Joseph Pulitzer to the rescue!

Pulitzer was a publisher living in New York City who believed the statue would be a symbol of freedom. He had a great idea. He asked everyone living in New York City to help pay for the statue. He put an ad in his newspaper, the *New York World*, and said, "We must raise the money!"

Anyone who donated would have their name published in the paper! Children, businessmen, politicians, and women donated! These were some of the names of the people who donated:

- Jonathan, 230 dollars
- Anna, 25 cents
- Ralph, 10 cents

▶ *Have you ever donated money for something you believed in? What was it, and how much did you give?*

HOORAY! On June 17, 1885, the pieces arrived in New York Harbor. There were 350 pieces, all packed into over 200 wooden crates.

THE SYMBOLISM OF THE STATUE OF LIBERTY HAS BEEN USED TO PROMOTE MANY CAUSES, SUCH AS WAR BONDS FOR WORLD WAR I

Remember Your First Thrill of AMERICAN LIBERTY

YOUR DUTY-Buy United States Government Bonds 2nd Liberty Loan of 1917

UNVEIL IT!

Look at the Statue of Liberty!

When it was unveiled on October 28, 1886, it was the tallest iron structure in the world:

- Without the base: 151 feet and one inch.
- With the base: 305 feet and one inch.

The United States cheered for this wonderful gift from their friends in France. Today, there are replicas of it all over the world. One of the most famous is in Paris, France, less than a mile downriver from the Eiffel Tower!

In 1906, the Army Corps of Engineers installed an elevator to take people all the way up to the top.

Be careful, it's a tight squeeze in there!

Joseph Pulitzer's son Ralph also raised money to set up a lighting system. The statue stood tall during the day and shone over the city at night. In 1923, President Calvin Coolidge declared the statue a national monument!

Many immigrants who traveled across the ocean to live in America saw the statue as they arrived. It was a beautiful sign of freedom and new opportunities.

The design team had to overcome many challenges, including finding a way to ship the statue all the way from France to the United States. But after all their hard work and some extra fundraising, they were able to **BUILD IT!**

SCIENCE SAFETY

Did you know the Statue of Liberty gets hit by six hundred bolts of lightning every year? Yikes!

DESIGN DETAIL

She has big feet! Her shoe size is 879. What is your shoe size?

The Eiffel Tower

THE PROBLEM!

Bonjour, Paris!

In 1885, Paris, France, was the world's capital of music, technology, and art. It was an exciting time! Composer Claude Debussy was studying and writing music and painter Claude Monet was a leader of the *impressionist* movement.

In 1871, there was a violent battle in the city. The people of Paris tried to form a new government called the Paris Commune, and fought against the existing French government. Look at the destruction on the Rue de Rivoli, where many street fights took place.

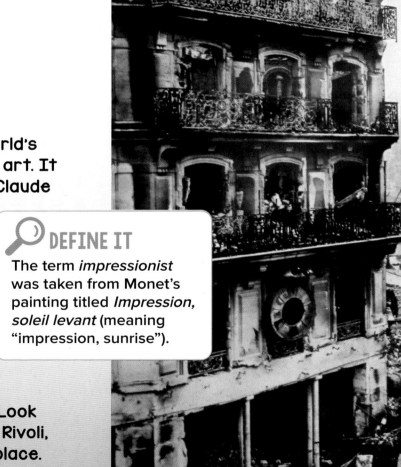

DEFINE IT

The term *impressionist* was taken from Monet's painting titled *Impression, soleil levant* (meaning "impression, sunrise").

Over a decade later, the city was still rebuilding! It would take a long time to clean up the streets and fix all the homes that were destroyed.

But Paris had a BIG problem!

In 1889, Paris was going to host the *Exposition Universelle*—a world's fair! The fair was a huge celebration of food, dance, invention, and music. People all over the world were going to travel to this exciting city. Many other cities had already hosted a world's fair, and each had created a unique structure to welcome visitors. Everyone had loved the Crystal Palace built for the fair in London in 1851! The city leaders needed a beautiful entrance to welcome visitors. What would they build?

IT'S HISTORY!

The exposition was planned for the one hundredth anniversary of the storming of the Bastille, one of the events that started the French Revolution. WATCH OUT! The fortress is crumbling!

THE SOLUTION!

A tower!

It would've been wonderful to have a beautiful centerpiece in the city of Paris. But what could they build that would be perfect for the world's fair?

THE TEAM!

The city leaders needed a great team to create a design for the tower. This included:

- *Engineers* to decide the perfect height, width, and length for the structure.
- *Financiers* to pay for the project.
- *Builders* to make sure it would not collapse.

BUDGET IT!

In 1886, the president of France, Jules Grévy, and the minister for trade, Édouard Lockroy, said they would pay as long as the tower:

- Had four sides and a square base.
- Was at least one thousand feet tall.

Over one hundred people sent in their ideas! Finally, the leaders picked . . .

ENGINEERING EXTRA
Did you know that Gustave Eiffel also designed the interior of the Statue of Liberty, and tried to help France build the Panama Canal decades before the United States did?

GUSTAVE EIFFEL

Gustave Eiffel!

Gustave Eiffel was an engineer who had a large company in Paris. He said he could build the tallest tower in the world! The leaders gave him 1.5 million francs to build the tower. That would be over 8 million dollars today!

He asked two engineers who worked for his company to join his team. Maurice Koechlin and Émile Nouguier drew a tower with *lattices* and four equal sides. The original blueprint was inspired by the Latting

Observatory in New York City—another world's fair centerpiece.

Even though he didn't draw the original design, Gustave Eiffel bought the sketches from his engineers. He also got a patent. This made sure no one else could copy his idea.

> 🔍 **DEFINE IT**
>
> A *lattice* is a design made up of overlapping lines with small gaps in the middle. It's the same as the pattern on a waffle!

AD FOR LATTING OBSERVATORY

OBSERVATORY SALOON

42d STREET,

Opposite the Crystal Palace,

NEW YORK.

E. GREENFIELD & CO.

Would give notice to the public that they have fitted up the second floor of the

LATTING OBSERVATORY

AS A LADIES'

Ice Cream & Refreshment

SALOON,

Where they are now prepared to serve ladies and gentlemen with

BREAKFAST, DINNER AND TEA,

And all the various kinds of refreshments of the best the market affords.

Private Parties served on the shortest notice.

N. B.—This is the largest and best ventilated Saloon in the city. "extending from 42d to 43d streets, 200 feet in depth.

ENTRANCE ON 42d STREET.

E. GREENFIELD & CO.

New York, July 12th, 1853.

Baker, Godwin & Co., Printers, Tribune Buildings 1 Spruce Street, New York.

DESIGN IT!

The French leaders wanted to change some of the tower's design elements. Even though it was tall, they wanted to make sure the tower looked beautiful, too. They needed . . .

An architect!

The leaders asked Stephen Sauvestre to add to the blueprint. He drew big arches and glass walls on every level.

Eiffel also added three levels for visitors, an observation deck, and 1,665 steps. That is a lot to climb! So, the design team also added *elevators*.

▶ *How many levels would you have made?*

When the people of France saw the design . . .

ELEVATORS TO THE OBSERVATION DECK

They hated it!

The newspapers said it was terrible! Artists from around Paris signed a petition. They did not want their beautiful city to be ruined with an ugly structure. People called the tower "monstrous" and "hideous."

But Eiffel and his team knew they could build the tallest and most beautiful tower in the world. So they kept designing.

NAME IT!

Gustave Eiffel was very clever. Because he bought the design and obtained the patent for it, he got to name the tower after himself. He named it . . .

the **Eiffel Tower!**

▶ *Fill in the blank with your last name. If you owned the Eiffel Tower, it would be called . . .*
the _____ Tower!

CITY FACT
In French, the Eiffel Tower is called *la Tour Eiffel.* It is also nicknamed the "Iron Lady."

Der Eiffelthurm und die Hauptanlagen der Parifer Weltausstellung 1889.

BUILD IT!

Let the digging begin!

On January 28, 1887, construction began.

The metal pieces of the tower and the rivets were brought into Paris. Rivets are fasteners that are pounded into place while they're red hot. They get smaller when they cool down, making a super-tight fit. The rivets made sure that the tower would stay in place!

SCIENCE SAFETY

Two of the tower's foundations had to be built close to the Seine River. The ground there was so muddy that water kept leaking in! The workers built a *caisson*, or chamber, that kept the water out until they could dig deep enough to find solid ground.

ENGINEERING EXTRA

Did you know that the tower has over eighteen thousand pieces, which were carefully put together like a big puzzle?

Four builders were needed for each rivet:

- The first builder would heat the rivet, making it easy to shape.
- The second builder would hold it.
- The third builder would shape the top to make it round.
- The fourth builder would beat it into the tower with a hammer. *BANG!*

The workers had to hammer rivets for hours. Their legs and arms ached as sparks flew around them. The metal screeched like a bat in a cave. People watching said it looked like there was a cloud of smoke in the Paris sky.

Oh no!

The exposition was starting!

Visitors had to climb over six hundred steps to get from the first floor to the second. It was exciting to be so high above Paris! But the elevators had not yet been built. The workers did not give up. They worked night and day to finish in less than a month so people could reach the observation deck.

FINISHING TOUCHES!

The Eiffel Tower was quickly painted a deep red-brown color. This was so the metal would not corrode or fade in the strong winds of Paris.

▶ *What color would you paint the tower, and why?*

DESIGN DETAIL
Today, there are two restaurants in the Eiffel Tower! You can eat buttery croissants, sweet crème brûlée, and soft crepes. Yum!

DESIGN DETAIL
Did you know the tower was painted yellow ten years after it opened? This was to fight rust. The color was later changed to a mix of yellow-brown that is called "Eiffel Tower Brown."

UNVEIL IT!

Look at the Eiffel Tower!

Even though the citizens of France originally hated the idea, the Eiffel Tower was a huge success at the world's fair. Two million people came from all over the world to admire the tower's height and beauty.

When it opened on March 31, 1889, it was:

- The tallest structure in the world: 984 feet.
- One of the heaviest towers in the world: 10,000 tons.

The Eiffel Tower took only two years to build and was supposed to stand for 20 years. After the end of the world's fair, the city leaders wanted to tear it down. But in 1898, Gustave Eiffel had an idea! He added an antenna to the top of the tower.

The Eiffel Tower became a radio! Eiffel showed everyone that the tower was tall, beautiful, and useful, too. It is still used as a radio and communication antenna today.

The Eiffel Tower is the most visited paid-admission landmark in the world. It is also a symbol of romance! Many people stand under the tower and kiss someone they love.

The design team overcame many challenges, but after all the hard work, they were able to **BUILD IT!**

ENGINEERING EXTRA

Did you know that the Eiffel Tower grows six inches in the summer and shrinks in the winter because of the pressure on the iron? That is half the size of a ruler!

The Panama Canal

Panama, 1914

THE PROBLEM!

In the nineteenth century, countries all around the world were *trading* important goods and merchandise with one another. These included tea, silk, pepper, lumber, and leather!

How do *you* think the countries around the world exchanged goods at this time?

A. Plane

B. Ship

C. Car

D. Rocket

If you picked *B*, you're right!

> 🔍 **DEFINE IT**
>
> *Trade* is when people buy and sell materials.

Ships were the most important form of transportation for trade, but their voyages were long and difficult. If England wanted to trade luxury clothing for colorful spices from Chile, ships would have to travel across the Atlantic Ocean, then down and around the southern tip of South America.

The water rocked the ship back and forth. Thunderstorms made the waves grow higher and stronger! *SPLASH! Water was everywhere!* People got seasick and ships were damaged.

What could make trading easier?

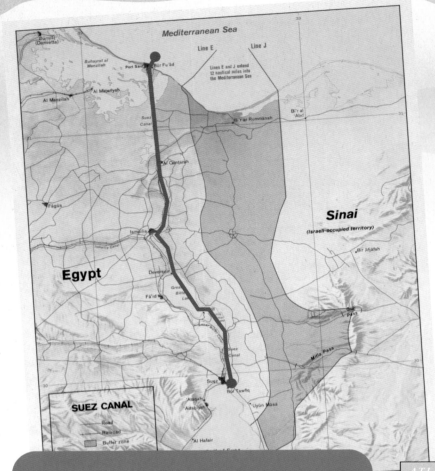

THE SOLUTION!

In 1881, Ferdinand de Lesseps, a French diplomat and leader, had a great idea. He could build a canal!

His company had already built the Suez Canal, which connected the Mediterranean Sea to the Red Sea and Indian Ocean.

The leaders of France were very excited about the idea of a *new* canal. They set a budget of 237 million dollars. De Lesseps asked his friend Gustave Eiffel to help design *locks* for the canal.

 **DEFINE IT**
Locks are chambers of water that fill or drain to raise or lower ships.

MATH FACT

Before the Suez Canal, ships going from Mumbai, India, to London, England, had to travel 12,300 miles. Using the Suez Canal, they only had to travel 7,200 miles. How many fewer miles did they have to travel?

IT'S HISTORY!

The idea for a canal actually started in the sixteenth century, when the Spanish explorer Vasco Núñez de Balboa discovered that Panama was an *isthmus* that separated the Atlantic and Pacific Oceans!

 **DEFINE IT**
An *isthmus* is a narrow piece of land separating two bodies of water.

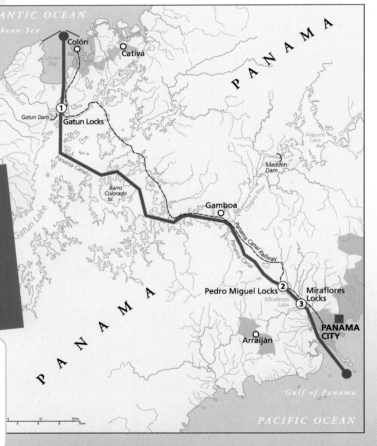

What other structures did Eiffel help to build?

A. The Statue of Liberty
B. The Burj Khalifa
C. The Golden Gate Bridge
D. The Eiffel Tower

If you picked *A* and *D*, you're right!

Builders started digging the canal right away. Large rocks and mud were piled up on the sides.

Watch out!

The ground was wet and muddy from tropical storms. Landslides covered the path. People got hurt. Some were buried under the dirt.

After thirteen years, thousands of people had died and millions of dollars had been spent.

The leaders of France said *NO MORE!* De Lesseps and Eiffel were fired for poor planning and wasting the country's money!

SCIENCE SAFETY
Many of the workers also got sick with malaria and yellow fever. At the time, they didn't realize the illnesses were passed by mosquito bites!

In 1902, US president Theodore Roosevelt bought the land from France for 40 million dollars. He hoped that a canal would make the US *economy* stronger.

THE TEAM!

President Roosevelt hired John Stevens to be the chief engineer. He was an expert at designing railroads. Dr. William Gorgas, the chief sanitary officer of the US Army, was hired to keep the area safe and clean for workers.

BUDGET IT!

The United States said the canal would cost around 375 million dollars. That would be close to 9 billion dollars today!

US PRESIDENT THEODORE ROOSEVELT

NAME IT!

In 1903, the country of Panama declared its independence from Colombia. Since the canal was going to be built through Panama, it was called the Panama Canal!

▶ *Fill in the blank with the name of the country or city you live in. It would be called... the _____ Canal!*

MATH FACT
Every ship that passes has to pay a toll. The smallest toll ever paid was only 38 cents. Some of the largest ships have to pay thousands of dollars!

DESIGN IT!

Designing the canal was no easy task. It needed to:

- Be 40 miles long.
- Be safe for ships that were 100 feet wide.
- Cut through the continental divide (a major mountain range).
- Dig through thick foliage in the jungle.

Stevens looked at the land and decided they should use railways to excavate the rocks, dirt, and mud. This would prevent landslides! He also designed a system of locks that would open and close, letting water flow in and out. The water would help carry the ships through the canal.

BUILD IT!

Builders came from the Caribbean, Spain, and the United States. Stevens made sure that the builders and their families had homes, schools, and even hospitals! The terrain was very difficult to work on, but finally the path was laid.

Dr. Gorgas conducted tests on the old water that collected in pools around the rocks, and he observed that the mosquitoes who gathered there were making people sick. He drained all the old water to help prevent the spread of disease.

After working on the canal for two years, Stevens suddenly got frustrated and said, "I QUIT!" No one knew why he left. The project needed a new team leader.

George Washington Goethels, a US Army general and civil engineer, was made the new head of construction. There was still a lot of work to be done!

Builders worked on both sides of the isthmus. It was very hot and sticky outside. The temperature reached one hundred degrees Fahrenheit!

Goethels made the workers dig nonstop. The sounds of the canal were loud!

BOOM! as dynamite exploded.

DRRRRR! as drills pushed into the ground.

WHOOSH! as steam trains carried rocks away.

▶ *Would you rather work with the dynamite, the drills, or the trains? Why?*

SCIENCE SAFETY
On the Pacific side, the river started to flood. Engineers constructed a dike—a long wall—so the builders could keep working without drowning.

The builders flooded one section of the path to create Gatun Lake, which sat almost 80 feet above sea level. At the time, it was the largest man-made lake in the world.

But something important was missing . . .

FINISHING TOUCHES!

The locks!

Locks were built on both sides of the canal. When a ship entered, the locks closed and the water level rose or fell to match the next section of the canal. Once the locks opened again on the other side, the ship could exit.

DESIGN DETAIL
The locks look like a wall that would protect a castle or fortress. These are very different from the locks you would use to open a door with a key!

UNVEIL IT!

In 1914, the Panama Canal officially opened!

This great feat of engineering:

- Took ten years to build.
- Was 40 miles long.
- Cut travel time across the world in half.

On August 15, 1914, the SS *Ancon* became the first ship to pass through the canal. The journey took only ten hours!

Today, almost one million ships have traveled the canal.

The United States controlled the canal until 1999, when that power was given over to Panama. This was after many years of protests and negotiations.

SS ANCON

The United States still uses the canal more than any other country in the world.

Even though it cost millions of dollars, thousands of people died, many people quit, and it took more than thirty years to finish, they were finally able to **BUILD IT!**

IT'S HISTORY!

In 1994, the American Society of Civil Engineers declared the Panama Canal one of the Seven Wonders of the *Modern World*. Other structures on this important list include the CN Tower in Canada and the Golden Gate Bridge in California.

ENGINEERING EXTRA

The steel used for the Golden Gate Bridge was transported from Philadelphia through the Panama Canal to San Francisco!

67

The Golden Gate Bridge

San Francisco, United States, 1937

THE PROBLEM!

In 1917, San Francisco was one of the largest cities in the United States. Thousands of people had rushed there in search of gold! Other people came for the cool, windy weather by San Francisco Bay. San Francisco was also an important shipping center. Ferries would come in and out of the city carrying people and delivering goods. Ferries were the only

SAN FRANCISCO HOUSES BUILT BETWEEN 1849 AND 1915

way people could travel between San Francisco and Sausalito, on the other side of the bay, to get to their jobs and visit friends.

The ferry ride across the bay was twenty minutes long.

The wind was strong and blustery! The ferry rocked back and forth. People almost fell overboard!

It was also expensive. The ferry cost one dollar! One dollar in 1917 would be more than 20 dollars today!

People worried because the United States was spending a lot of money fighting in World War I.

There needed to be an easier and less expensive way to connect the two cities.

THE SOLUTION!

The people of San Francisco began talking about building a bridge. A bridge would:

- Make travel faster.
- Give construction workers jobs.
- Cost less money to enter and exit the city.

But bridges are very expensive and difficult to construct. San Francisco and Sausalito are over five thousand feet apart, separated by San Francisco Bay and the Golden Gate Strait.

▶ *How are a* bay *and a* strait *similar and different?*

> ## 🔍 DEFINE IT
> A *bay* is a body of water surrounded by land with only one opening. A *strait* is a narrow passage of water that connects two other bodies of water.

The shallow parts of the Golden Gate Strait are 15 feet deep. The deepest part is 350 feet. The workers would have to dive in!

The strait was home to many different species of animals. Sharks, sea otters, and bat rays swam deep in the cold waters. Some could be deadly if they attacked. The bay had strong, wild winds and unpredictable fog. This made it hard to see. The water in the strait was cold, ran fast, and slammed against the coastline. On the shore, it was windy and wet.

How could they build in this weather?

THE TEAM!

By 1923, the state leaders were ready to build and needed a great team. This included:

- An *engineer* to decide the perfect height and length for the bridge.
- An *architect* to design a beautiful bridge.
- A *builder* to construct material strong enough to withstand the weather.
- A *financier* to pay for the project.

▶ *If you were on the team, what role would you want to play, and why?*

BUDGET IT!

The state leaders had no idea how to build a huge bridge. Then they had an idea:

A competition!

They wanted to find someone who could create the best design for the least amount of money. The winner would be given the money to design and build! James Wilkins, an engineer, asked for 100 million dollars. Joseph B. Strauss, an engineer and poet, asked for approximately 20 million dollars.

The winner was . . .

Joseph B. Strauss! He had designed over four hundred drawbridges! As the team leader, he also got a salary of 1 million dollars. That would be over 20 million dollars today!

JOSEPH B. STRAUSS (RIGHT)

DESIGN IT!

The design team drew the blueprint. Should the bridge be tall or short? Wide or narrow?

Strauss's first blueprint was a cantilever-suspension hybrid bridge. This type of bridge has two large cantilevers, or angled support frames, on each side, and suspended cables in the middle.

When people saw the drawing of the bridge . . .

They hated it!

The newspaper wrote that it looked ugly. The bridge got a new nickname . . .

The IMPOSSIBLE Bridge!

The city was also worried about earthquakes. There had been a big earthquake in San Francisco in 1906. Buildings crumbled to the ground and parks burned in a blazing fire. Look at that smoke! Everyone was worried. If there was another earthquake, would the bridge collapse?

SMOKE FROM THE
SAN FRANCISCO FIRE, 1906

Another engineer on the team, Leon Moisseiff, had a new idea! He drew a suspension bridge. His design used concrete, steel, and cables.

A suspension bridge could withstand the harsh weather. The cables would allow the suspension bridge to slowly sway from side to side in heavy winds. The architect, Irving Morrow, added elements of art deco to the design. Art deco was a very popular style of architecture in the early twentieth century. It made the bridge beautiful.

Everyone was excited. The design was done!

NAME IT!

The design team wanted to pick a unique name so people would get excited about the bridge.

In 1846, a US Army officer named John C. Frémont had visited the strait and named it *Chrysopylae*, a Greek word that means "golden gate." Because the bridge was going to pass over the Golden Gate Strait, everyone decided that the Golden Gate Bridge was the best name!

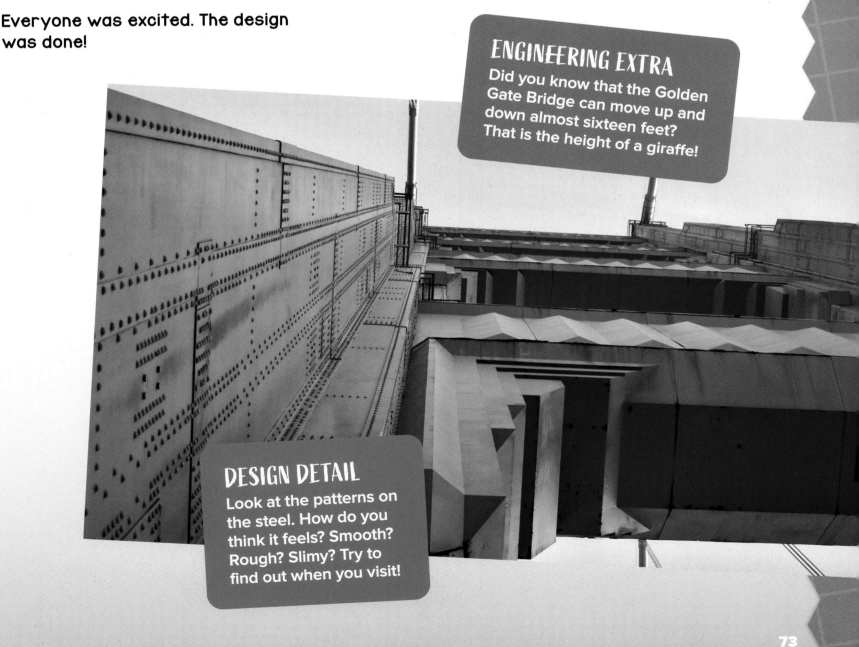

ENGINEERING EXTRA
Did you know that the Golden Gate Bridge can move up and down almost sixteen feet? That is the height of a giraffe!

DESIGN DETAIL
Look at the patterns on the steel. How do you think it feels? Smooth? Rough? Slimy? Try to find out when you visit!

BUILD IT!

Digging day! On January 5, 1933, the excavators dug into the mud. The construction workers put on their hard hats and glare-free goggles.

The builders worked in two parallel teams—one in each city.

Big pits were created for the two tall towers that would hold the bridge over the water. Large pieces of steel traveled by ship from New Jersey, down through the Panama Canal, and up to San Francisco. The towers were both built at the same time, to support the large suspension cables that draped across the strait.

The winds got stronger, and the water splashed faster. There was no place for the builders to stand! They had two choices to survive: balance on the steel or hang from ropes.

It was like being on a high wire in a circus!

Because of the strong winds, building the Golden Gate Bridge was especially hard. On February 17, 1937, ten workers

SCIENCE SAFETY
Glare-free goggles helped the workers see. The water in the strait was so bright, it was like looking directly at the sun! If they weren't careful, they could go blind.

DESIGN DETAIL
Did you know that there are five plaques on the bridge? These were dedicated to the construction workers and the design team. Try to find them when you visit!

died when they fell through broken scaffolding that was supposed to hold them up and keep them safe. Today, there are more safety laws to protect workers.

Deep in the water

Designing a bridge over the strait meant that builders had to be working above the water and . . .

UNDERWATER!

The divers had an important job.

BOOM!

Dynamite blasted debris and made space for underwater concrete walls. The walls protected the area from fast currents that could pull the divers out to sea.

FINISHING TOUCHES!

The paint color for the bridge had to protect the steel against corrosion from salt water that slammed against it. The bridge also had to stand out against the colors of the California coastline and the thick San Francisco fog.

The US Navy wanted to paint the bridge yellow and black. The US Army Air Corps wanted to paint the bridge red and white. Imagine how the bridge might have looked with stripes!

▶ *What color would you choose to paint the bridge, and why?*

The design team finally chose the color "international orange." This was an exciting and useful color for the Golden Gate Bridge. It would help prevent corrosion and stand out in the fog.

SCIENCE SAFETY

International orange is a popular color for designing space suits, because it can be seen very easily when you land your space capsule in the ocean!

UNVEIL IT!

The Golden Gate Bridge was officially opened on May 27, 1937!

People applauded and cheered!

Everyone was excited to have a new way to travel across the strait, and it cost only 50 cents to drive across. It took four years and 35 million dollars to build the Golden Gate Bridge.

When it opened, it was:

- The longest bridge in the world, at 4,200 feet.
- The tallest bridge in the world, at 746 feet.

Every day, thousands of cars cross the Golden Gate Bridge. It is an important structure in the United States and became a California historical landmark on June 18, 1987.

The design team overcame many challenges, including the strong winds and deep waters, but after all the hard work, they were able to **BUILD IT!**

CITY FACT
On its opening day, people could walk across the bridge for free!

IT'S HISTORY!
Remember that Joseph B. Strauss was an engineer *and* a poet? He wrote a poem about the bridge when it was finally complete: "The Mighty Task Is Done"!

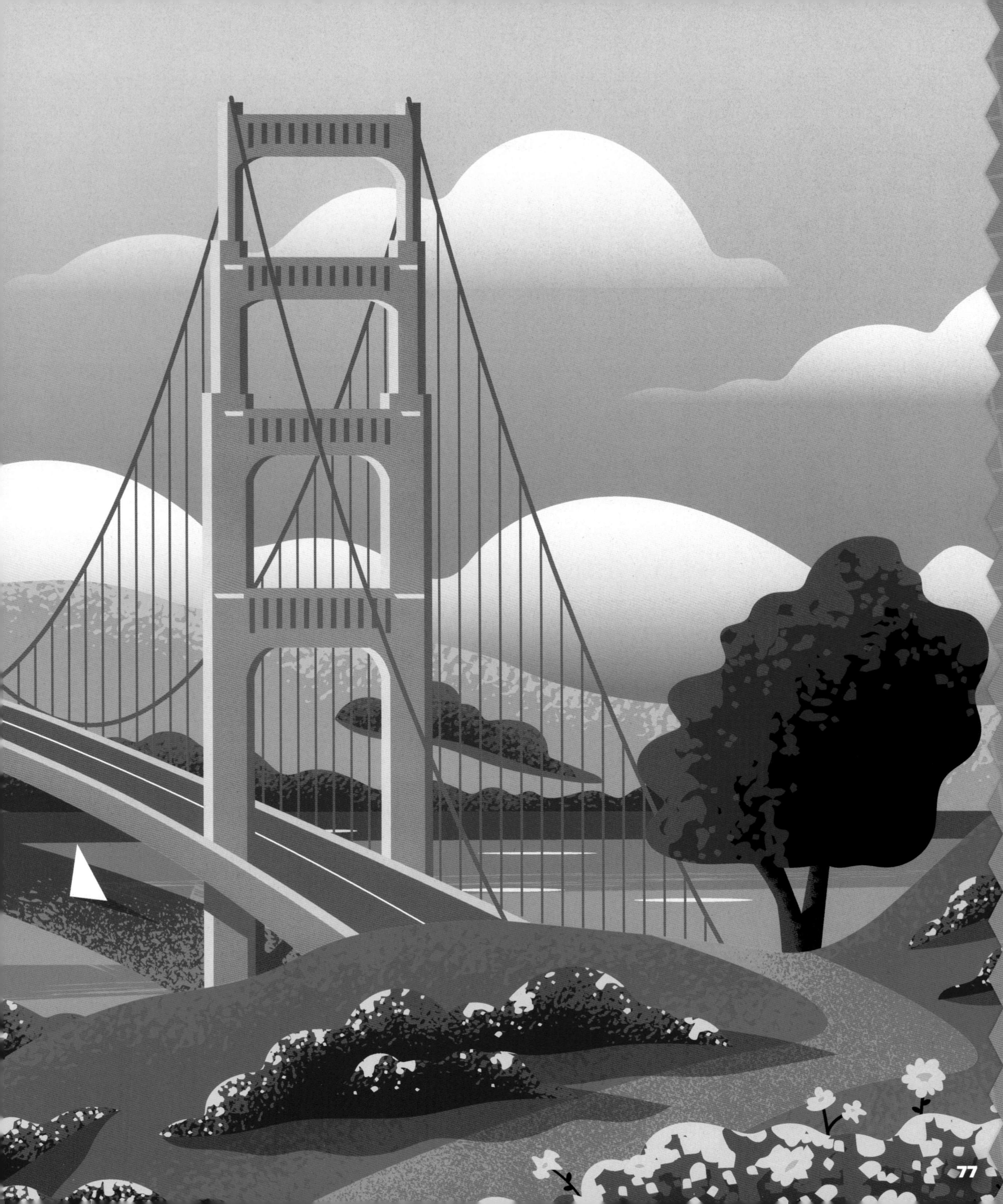

The Sydney Opera House

Sydney, Australia, 1973

THE PROBLEM!

In the 1950s, Sydney was a beautiful, warm coastal city that had the biggest and safest harbor in Australia. Many people came to visit during the Royal Easter Show. There was an agriculture parade and a wood-chopping contest!

There were also a lot of musical events. Sir Eugene Goossens moved to Australia to conduct the Sydney Symphony Orchestra. Originally from London, he had been a conductor all over the United States.

When he went to rehearse, he found that the big orchestra was supposed to perform in a small town hall. He asked the New South Wales premier, Joseph Cahill, to help them find a bigger space.

Why do you think he needed a bigger space for the orchestra?

A. He wanted to have more seats for the audience.

B. He wanted to build an opera company.

C. He wanted a concert hall just for the symphony.

D. All of the above.

If you picked D, you're right!

In 1954, Cahill made an important announcement. He said he would build a new performance space to "help mould a better and more enlightened community."

But . . .

Cahill had a BIG problem!

Sydney was a bustling city with a lot of buildings and homes. Where could they build?

THE SOLUTION!

Bennelong Point!

Sydney's harbor was an important place. The Gadigal people of the Eora Nation called it *Tubowgule*, meaning "where the knowledge waters meet." This was a place of celebration and gathering for many, many years.

The land was named after Woollarawarre Bennelong, a respected Eora man who had been kidnapped by the first governor of New South Wales. He helped the governor communicate with the Eora people. He did such a good job that when he asked for land to build a hut, the governor said *YES!*

A tram depot was still sitting on the land. *What could the city leaders do?*

Demolish it!

The tram depot was broken down and was removed to make way for the new structure.

WOOLLARAWARRE BENNELONG

IT'S HISTORY!
Many different buildings stood on Bennelong Point over the years. This included Bennelong's hut, a theater, a fort, and a tram depot!

THE TEAM!

By 1956, Cahill needed to find:

- A *designer* to create a beautiful blueprint and outline for the structure.
- *Engineers* to make sure the design was safe.
- *Builders* to help with construction.

So, he held . . .

A contest!

Four judges looked at each of the entries. There were 222 designs from twenty-eight different countries. At the very last minute, one more architect sent in his design.

Jørn Utzon was a Danish architect. He sent in twelve drawings the night before the competition ended.

The judges loved how Utzon's drawings looked like sails on the edge of the Australian waters. Utzon's design used all of the shoreline and did not waste any space. He also made sure that the building would be beautiful from every angle. The judges said the design would be *controversial* because it was so unique and original.

 **DEFINE IT**

Controversial means something that people disagree about.

After the judges looked at all 223 designs, the winner was Utzon! He was thirty-eight years old when he won.

DESIGN DETAIL

This architectural style was called "expressionism." Expressionism focused more on form (what the building looked like) than function (what it was supposed to do). Expressionist buildings used beautiful shapes and looked like sculptures. Another expressionist building is the Guggenheim Museum in New York City.

BUDGET IT!

Cahill set a budget of 3.5 million pounds—that would be 64 million dollars today. But this was a big project! *Would the budget be enough?*

DESIGN IT!

He said he could have the structure built in just four years. The state leaders were excited. They planned for three stages of building:

- Stage one: the upper podium
- Stage two: the outer shells
- Stage three: the interior design and final construction

NAME IT!

It was easy to name the structure. Because it was going to be a performing arts center with a symphony, the leaders named it the Sydney Opera House before they even announced the contest.

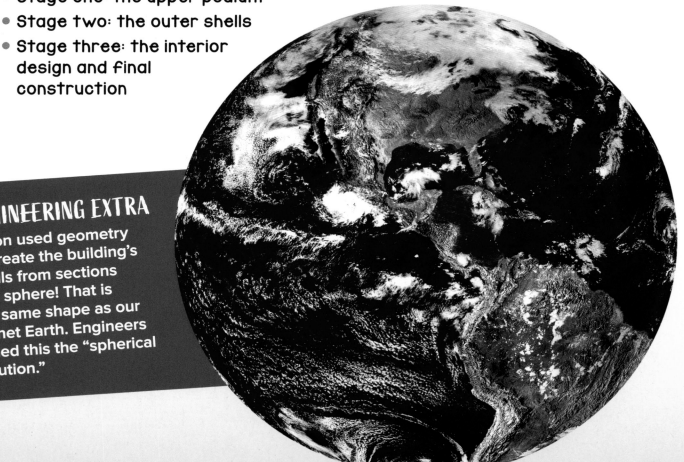

ENGINEERING EXTRA

Utzon used geometry to create the building's shells from sections of a sphere! That is the same shape as our planet Earth. Engineers called this the "spherical solution."

BUILD IT!

On March 2, 1959, Utzon arrived at the harbor with a bronze plaque. Cahill screwed it in, and the jackhammers started digging!

Stop!

Utzon said his design was not complete! He asked the builders to wait until he finished his design, but the leaders didn't listen and decided to start construction anyway.

In 1961, the construction was delayed. Strong storms and rain made it difficult to build and brought the threat of floods! Engineers on the team asked Utzon to change some of his original design. They were worried the sails would collapse. Utzon started to make revisions.

He changed his design again to include vaults and precast roofs. *Precast* means they were shaped before they were put into place.

The engineers loved it!

DESIGN DETAIL
The plaque is still on the steps of the Sydney Opera House. Try to find it when you visit and read what it says!

Using Utzon's design, more than two thousand concrete panels were shaped to look like shells. Each panel was precast and supported with concrete ribs—long, wide beams. They were designed to look just like the ribs in our bodies, which keep our heart and lungs safe! The ribs inside the shells would keep the structure safe and solid.

This new design helped to speed up the construction.

The year was now 1966. The builders had been working for seven years! The three main cranes arrived to shape the roof. Each crane cost 100,000 pounds.

MATH MEASUREMENT
How much did the cranes cost in total?

Utzon searched for the perfect tiles for the roof. He wanted the tiles to be shiny and glossy. He found a kind of tile in Sweden that took three years for artists to create from clay and stone. These are now called "Sydney Tiles."

FINISHING TOUCHES!

Utzon started working on stage three, the interior design. The original blueprint said there would be two theaters, but the state leaders now wanted four! They asked Utzon to change his design *again*! He got very frustrated, especially when the leaders also said they would not pay him for the extra work. So Utzon said,

"I QUIT!"

He left Australia, and the builders had to finish without him.

In the end, there were five performance spaces. Each was a different size.

They were called:

- The Concert Hall (2,679 seats)
- The Opera Theatre (1,547 seats)
- The Drama Theatre (544 seats)
- The Playhouse (398 seats)
- The Studio Theatre (364 seats)

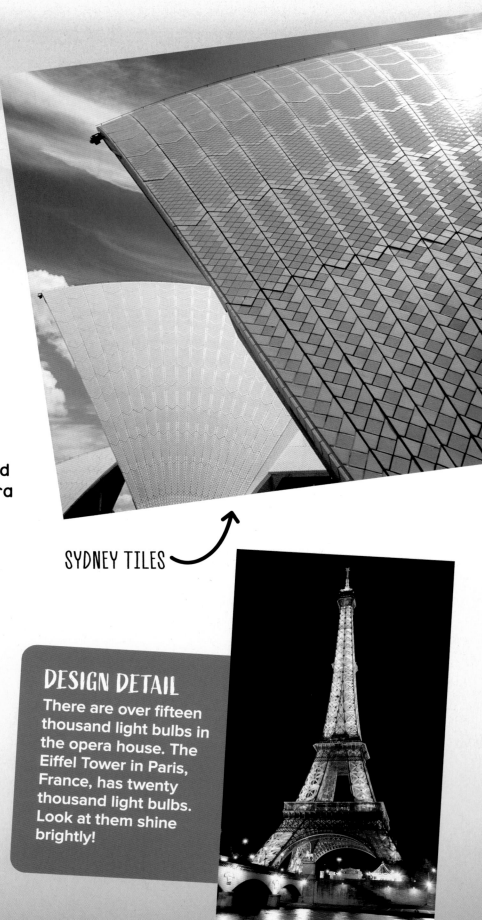

SYDNEY TILES

DESIGN DETAIL
There are over fifteen thousand light bulbs in the opera house. The Eiffel Tower in Paris, France, has twenty thousand light bulbs. Look at them shine brightly!

UNVEIL IT!

On October 20, 1973, Queen Elizabeth II officially opened the Sydney Opera House.

In the end, it:

- Took 14 years to build.
- Cost 102 million pounds.

Today, the opera house is the most visited landmark in Australia. Over 9 million people visit every year! In 2007, it was called a "masterpiece of creativity" by the UNESCO World Heritage Committee.

Some of the most famous musicians who have performed at the opera house include jazz singer Ella Fitzgerald and opera singer Joan Sutherland.

Although the cost was much more than expected, Utzon had to change his design many times, and eventually quit the project, they were able to **BUILD IT!**

IT'S HISTORY!
The year 2023 is the fiftieth anniversary of the opera house!

MUSIC MOMENT
It has the largest mechanical tracker-action organ in the world, with over ten thousand pipes.

The Vietnam Veterans Memorial

Washington, DC, United States, 1982

CITY FACT
The capital of South Vietnam was called Saigon. After North Vietnam won the war, and its government was in charge of all Vietnam, it changed the name to Ho Chi Minh City.

HO CHI MINH CITY TODAY

THE PROBLEM!

It was a difficult time in Vietnam. For over twenty years, soldiers across the country had been fighting for freedom. Many troops from the United States also fought in this long and difficult battle between North and South Vietnam.

The terrain was rough! Troops dressed in camouflage and waded deep into murky waters. Why do you think the troops wore camo?

    A. To have nice clothing.

    B. To blend in with the surroundings and hide from the enemy.

    C. Because it was hot!

If you picked *B*, you're right! Soldiers used camouflage to hide in the tall grass. This is the same way a chameleon can hide in a tree! *Can you find it?*

In 1975, the Vietnam War finally ended. Some soldiers were lucky to return home to their families, but many people had died during the battles.

The US government was grateful to all the soldiers who had fought.

What could they do to honor them and remember those who gave their lives?

IT'S HISTORY!

Many people were very angry that the Vietnam War even took place. During the war, there were protests all over the United States where people marched in the streets, shouting, *"END THE WAR NOW!"*

END THE WAR NOW

THE SOLUTION!

A memorial!

In 1979, Jan Scruggs, a *veteran* of the war, helped create the Vietnam Veterans Memorial Fund. This is an organization that collects *donations* to help the families of people who fought and died in the Vietnam War. It also raised money for a memorial dedicated to those veterans. Scruggs knew that a memorial would be a great way to honor and remember everyone who fought.

THE NATIONAL MALL AND
THE CONSTITUTION GARDENS

🔍 DEFINE IT

A *veteran* is someone who has a lot of experience in a certain field, or someone who has served in the military.

🔍 DEFINE IT

A *donation* is an amount of money given to an organization to help support a program or activity. There are many places where you can donate money or volunteer your own time! For example, donations could help:

- An animal hospital feed kittens and puppies.
- A sports team get new uniforms.
- A music class get new instruments to play.

But there were already three other memorials on the National Mall in Washington, DC. They honored presidents George Washington, Thomas Jefferson, and Abraham Lincoln.

Where could they build?

Scruggs and his team asked President Jimmy Carter to donate land from the Constitution Gardens. These gardens are a part of the National Mall that is just southwest of the White House.

President Carter said . . .

Yes!

He designated over two acres of land for building the memorial. That is the size of two football fields!

THE TEAM!

Scruggs and his colleagues at the fund knew they needed many people to make the memorial. This included:

- A *designer* to create a unique memorial that would reflect the war.
- An *engineer* to build the structure.

BUDGET IT!

The Vietnam Veterans Memorial Fund was already raising money to help build the structure—even though they didn't know what it would look like or how much it would cost. In five years, they collected over 9 million dollars!

DEFINE IT

The word *mall* means an open area for people to walk around in—it doesn't always mean a shopping mall!

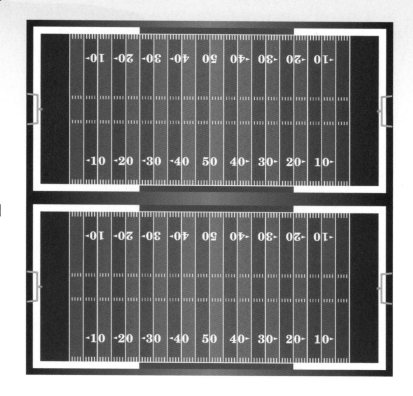

DESIGN IT!

Even though they had enough money to build a memorial, the leaders of the Vietnam Veterans Memorial Fund still did not have a design. So, they decided to have . . .

A competition!

Anyone who was eighteen years or older and a United States citizen could apply!

Each design had to follow four rules. It should:

1. Encourage people to reflect on why it was built.

2. Fit in with the surroundings.

3. Include the names of all the people who had died during the war, or who were still missing.

4. Not express a personal opinion about the war.

The memorial fund received 1,421 designs by the competition deadline of March 31, 1981. The judges were eight artists and designers. The designs were hung inside Andrews Air Force Base.

Each design had only a number—not the artist's name—so the judging would be anonymous and fair. The judges looked at each design, making sure it followed the four rules. Finally, they picked number…

1026!

The winning design was created by Maya Ying Lin. She was only twenty-one years old and had drawn the design as a class project! She was awarded 20,000 dollars for her design.

Lin wanted the memorial to be "a park within a park"— an area inside the Constitutional Gardens that was a quiet place to think about the war and the people who had fought. She drew two long triangles that met in the middle.

MAYA YING LIN'S WINNING DESIGN

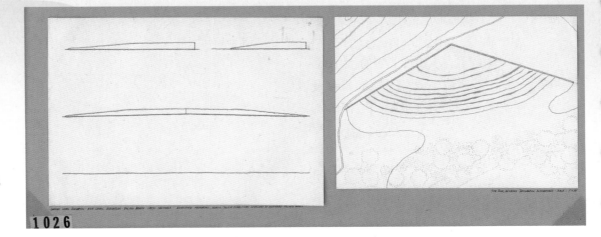

1026

The material she chose was polished black granite—it was shiny and reflected the trees and flowers that swayed in the gardens.

But some people did not like Lin's design! They called it "ugly" and said it looked like a hole in the ground. People also did not like the color she chose, saying that black was a dark and sad color. Still, Lin believed in her design and did not change her winning idea.

DESIGN DETAIL
Look at the material up close. *How do you think it feels? Smooth? Rough? Sticky?*

NAME IT!

Since it was going to honor the people who fought and died in the Vietnam War, the structure was called the Vietnam Veterans Memorial. It is also nicknamed "The Wall."

BUILD IT!

There were only three places in the world that had polished black granite. The United States got big slabs of granite from a quarry in Bengaluru, India. The granite was then shipped to Vermont, where each piece was cut and polished.

In Washington, DC, construction workers were busy digging up the ground to make the pathway for the wall. The workers dug 35 feet into the ground to make sure the walls would be stable and strong!

The walls were brought in and placed in the garden. But something was missing . . .

MATH FACT
At the vertex, where the walls meet, they are 10 feet, 1.5 inches high.

DESIGN DETAIL
Visitors can request a "name rubbing" on a piece of paper to take home.

FINISHING TOUCHES!

The names!

Each name was inscribed in the wall, starting with the first person who was known to have died in battle, or who remained missing. The letters for each name were made in a light gray color so they could be easily read against the shiny black granite.

The designers used a process called "photo stencil grit blasting." This is just like using a stencil to put one shape or image onto another material.

UNVEIL IT!

When it was finished, the Vietnam Veterans Memorial Wall:

- Had cost 8.4 million dollars.
- Had taken over three years to build.

Over 5 million people visit the memorial each year. It is a quiet space to reflect and think about how hard people fought during the war, and to respect the families who lost a loved one.

Even though the Vietnam War was a difficult battle and many lives were lost, the United States used Lin's winning design for a memorial and they were able to **BUILD IT!**

DESIGN DETAIL
More names have been added to the wall over the years, bringing the total number of names to 58,276.

The Burj Khalifa

Dubai, United Arab Emirates, 2010

THE PROBLEM!

Dubai was the busiest city in the United Arab Emirates. Thousands of people came from all over the world to see the modern buildings and experience the culture and cuisine. The city leaders wanted even more people to visit. They decided to expand the city center by building over thirty thousand homes and nine hotels.

The president was very excited. He asked his advisors: *Can we make something no one has ever done before?*

The city leaders wanted the development to have a centerpiece.

But they had a BIG problem!
What could they build that would impress everyone?

THE SOLUTION!

The tallest building in the world!

They wanted to build a tower that would have restaurants, apartments, hotels, and offices. They were very excited and started to look for a design team.

THE TEAM!

Adrian Smith was a famous architect and designer. He was part of the team that had designed Willis Tower in Chicago and One World Trade Center in New York City. The leaders of Dubai asked if he could create a unique design for the tallest tower in the world. And he said . . .

Yes!

He asked Nada Andric to be a designer on the team. She had won many awards for her ideas.

NADA ANDRIC

ADRIAN SMITH

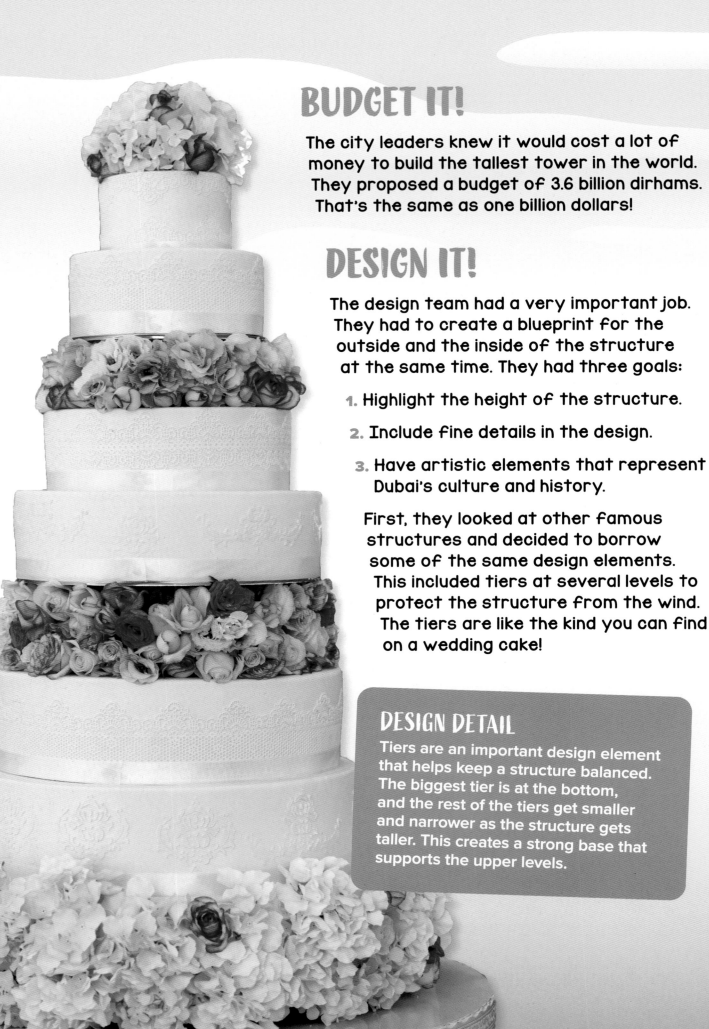

BUDGET IT!

The city leaders knew it would cost a lot of money to build the tallest tower in the world. They proposed a budget of 3.6 billion dirhams. That's the same as one billion dollars!

DESIGN IT!

The design team had a very important job. They had to create a blueprint for the outside and the inside of the structure at the same time. They had three goals:

1. Highlight the height of the structure.

2. Include fine details in the design.

3. Have artistic elements that represent Dubai's culture and history.

First, they looked at other famous structures and decided to borrow some of the same design elements. This included tiers at several levels to protect the structure from the wind. The tiers are like the kind you can find on a wedding cake!

DESIGN DETAIL

Tiers are an important design element that helps keep a structure balanced. The biggest tier is at the bottom, and the rest of the tiers get smaller and narrower as the structure gets taller. This creates a strong base that supports the upper levels.

Next, the architects wanted the building to represent the Middle Eastern desert. They used the desert flower *Hymenocallis* as the inspiration for the design.

The interior of the building would also have over 2 million square feet of space.

DESIGN DETAIL
Look at how the flower is the same shape as a bird's-eye view of the building!

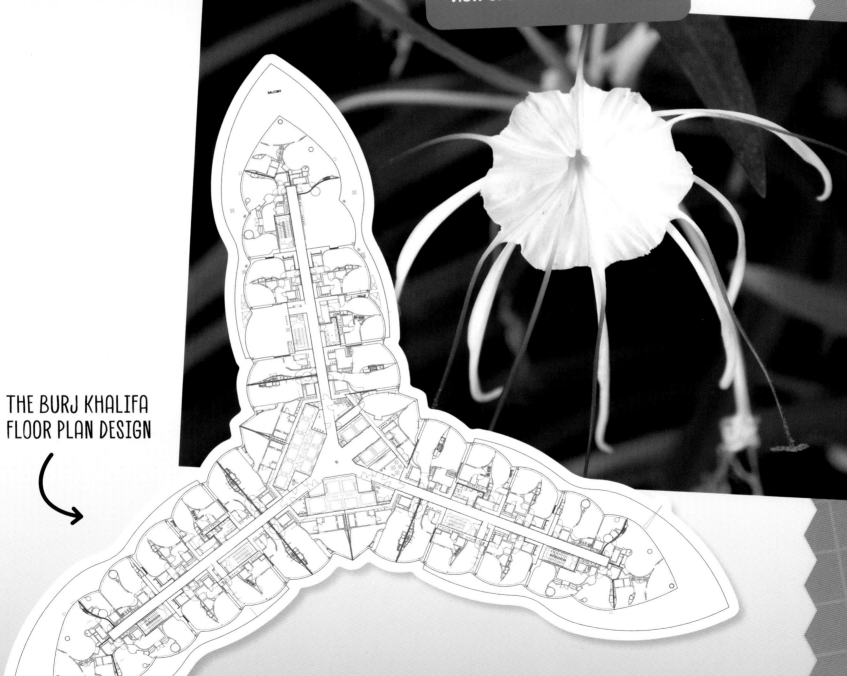

THE BURJ KHALIFA
FLOOR PLAN DESIGN

101

NAME IT!

The design team named the building the Burj Dubai. *Burj* means "tower" in Arabic. So while they were designing and getting ready to build, the structure was called the "Tower of Dubai."

▶ *But would the name change?*

BUILD IT!

In January 2004, the builders started digging.

First, the tower needed a lot of concrete and steel to create the base. The weight of the concrete was equal to 100,000 elephants, and the weight of the steel was equal to five airplanes!

The engineers and builders created a reinforced concrete skeleton to keep the tower strong in case there was an earthquake. Because the tower would stand in the hot desert sand, they had to drill and dig over 160 feet deep into the ground.

Oh no!

The rocks in the desert sand were very brittle and weak. Water started to rush into the drilled holes. The engineers used a material called *polymer* slurry to fill the holes and stop the water from spreading. The builders nicknamed the material "snot," since it looked like the mucus and boogers from our noses. *YUCK!*

DEFINE IT

Many kinds of plastic are *polymers*. They are used to make soccer balls, paint, and clothes hangers! *What do you have at home that uses polymers?*

SCIENCE SAFETY
The tower was built to withstand a 6.0 magnitude earthquake. That would be one of the most destructive earthquakes ever measured!

Next, the engineers conducted wind tunnel tests. They wanted to make sure the tower could withstand very strong winds without collapsing. *Phew!* The tower passed more than 40 safety tests!

The center of the tower is a hexagon protected by wings.

The wings have a concrete center that keeps them stable and strong. They also create a spiral that helps the building's shape become narrower as its height increases. This reduces the amount of wind that pushes against the building.

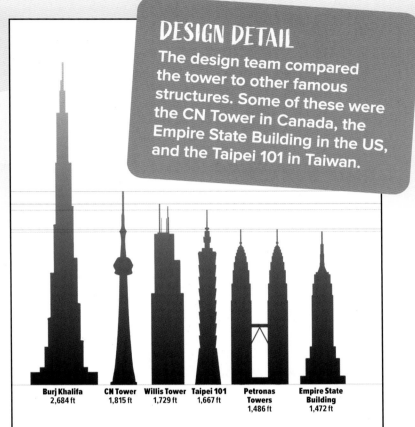

DESIGN DETAIL
The design team compared the tower to other famous structures. Some of these were the CN Tower in Canada, the Empire State Building in the US, and the Taipei 101 in Taiwan.

Burj Khalifa	CN Tower	Willis Tower	Taipei 101	Petronas Towers	Empire State Building
2,684 ft	1,815 ft	1,729 ft	1,667 ft	1,486 ft	1,472 ft

MATH FACT
Adding up the time for each individual person, the builders worked for 22 million hours!

FINISHING TOUCHES!

The main structure was finished! But at only 1,921 feet tall, it was still not the tallest tower in the world. The builders needed to hoist up the spire!

The builders used a hydraulic pump to push the spire into place. A hydraulic pump uses mechanical power to overcome the pressure of lifting something that is very heavy!

This is the same type of pump used on dump trucks and excavators.

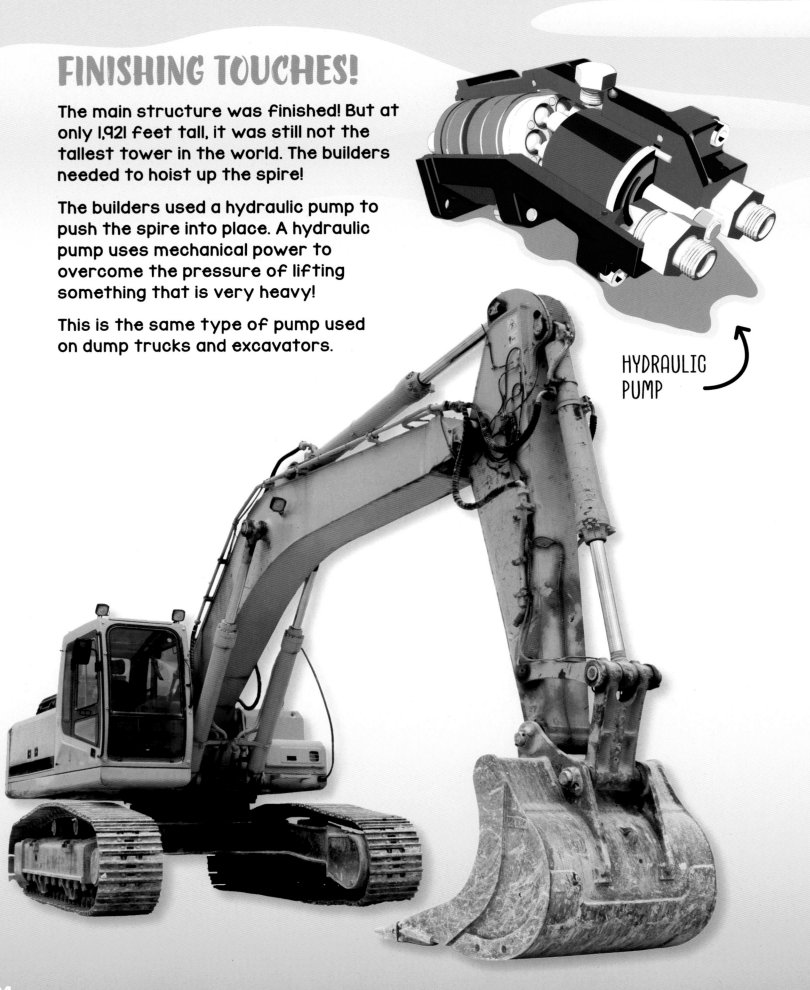

HYDRAULIC PUMP

CLICK! The spire was lifted and locked into place. It was 796 feet tall.

Add the tower height and the spire height. How tall is the tower?

A. 1,125 feet tall

B. 2,717 feet tall

C. 27,020 feet tall

If you picked *B*, you're right! The building was complete!

Now it was time to fill the inside of the structure with beautiful paintings. Nada Andric's finalized interior design included over 1,000 pieces of art!

ENGINEERING EXTRA

A spire is used on tall buildings and skyscrapers to make the building look nice, increase the height, or act as a lightning rod!

UNVEIL IT!

On January 4, 2010, the tower was ready to be opened to the public.

The design team wanted to honor the president of the United Arab Emirates, Sheikh Khalifa bin Zayed bin Sultan Al Nahyan. He gave a lot of money to Dubai. The money helped the design team finish building the tower.

So, they changed the name of the tower to the Burj Khalifa bin Zayed!

▶ *Fill in the blank with your first name! If the building were named after you, it would be called . . . the Burj _____ .*

When it was unveiled, the design team submitted their blueprints to the members of the Council on Tall Buildings and Urban Habitat. The Burj Khalifa was compared to other tall buildings around the world, such as One World Trade Center in New York City and the Shanghai Tower in China.

The Burj Khalifa was the new winner! It set many world records, including:

- Tallest human-made structure in the world (2,717 feet)
- Most stories (163 floors)
- Highest swimming pool (76th floor)
- Highest observation deck (1,823 feet)

Even though the city leaders had to create a design for the world's tallest tower, find a way to dig in the soft desert sand, and get extra money to finish the tower, they were able to **BUILD IT!**

🔍 **DEFINE IT**

Sheikh means "leader" in Arabic.

NAME FACT
This is different from how the Eiffel Tower was named, because Gustave Eiffel used his *last* name instead of his first!

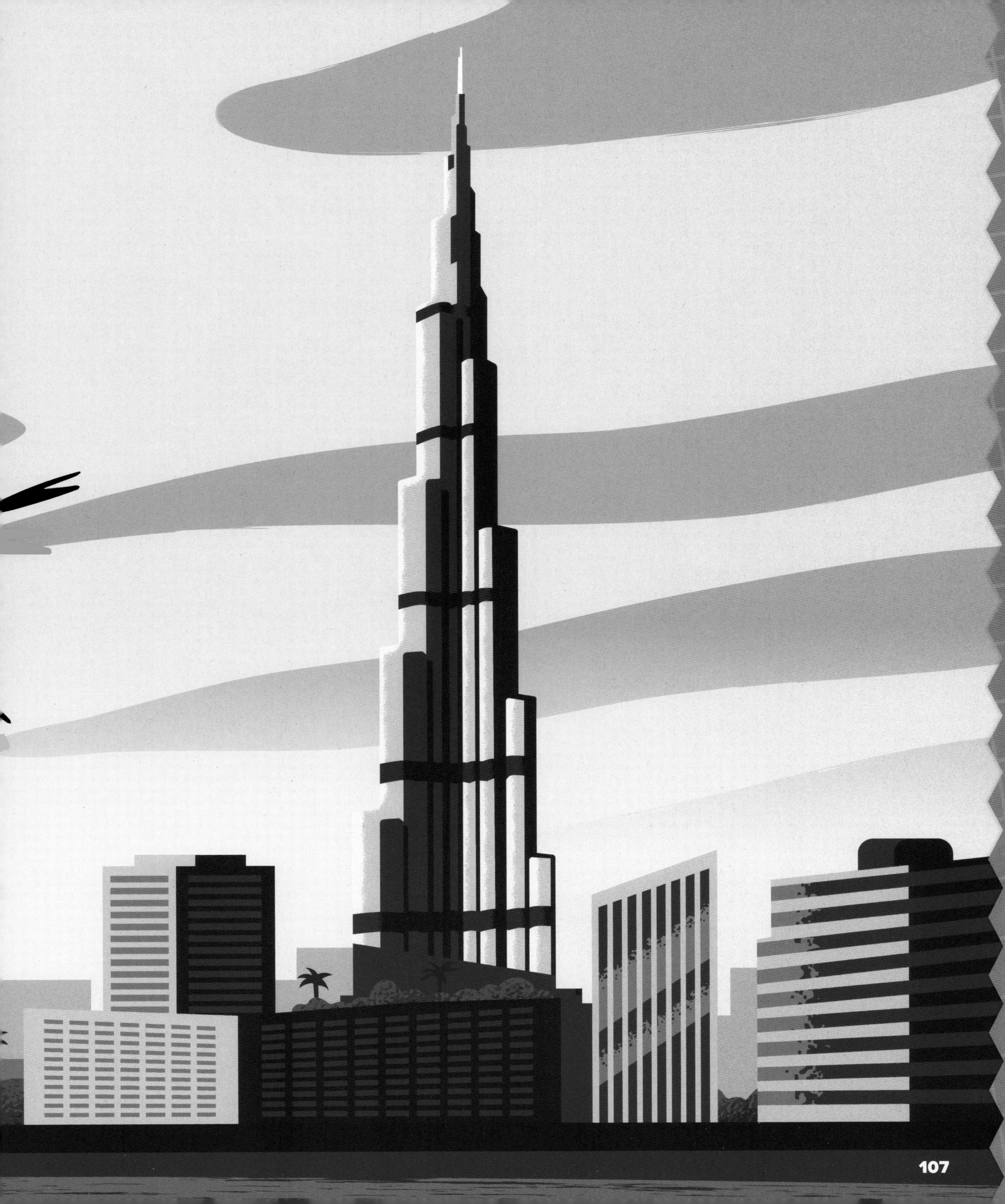

AUTHOR'S NOTE

Each of the ten landmarks in this collection is unique, interesting, and important to our world in different ways. Some were built and named for a person, others for a place, but each was designed with a specific purpose. The engineers and designers had many challenges to overcome, including finding the right materials, putting a team together, and, often, getting the community to agree that each landmark should be constructed!

The work of building the landmarks presented here spans over 2,000 years. And each year, more new landmarks and structures are designed and constructed all over the world. When selecting which ones to include in this collection, there were many that I had to leave out—hoping to at least highlight structures that represented a variety of cultures, countries, and artistic elements. There are many, many more that I would have loved to include and I still hope to write about.

Have you visited any of these landmarks? Which would you want to visit first? Next? When you do, take a picture, write a story about your visit, and think about how you would change the design! Then, please share it with me at Rekha_Rajan@att.net, on Twitter at RekhaSRajan, or on my website, RekhaSRajan.com.

I look forward to hearing from you and learning about what landmark you might create as a future engineer, architect, designer, builder, or scientist!

Rekha S. Rajan

ACKNOWLEDGMENTS

I recognize how lucky I am to launch my debut children's book with Scholastic. I am so grateful to my brilliant editor, Katie Heit, for recognizing the importance of having STEM and STEAM books on the market and for being an absolute joy to work with on this project. Every edit you gave was exactly what I would have made. I am incredibly grateful to the entire team at Scholastic, who loved, supported, and championed this project from the start.

When I shared the idea for this project with my amazing agent, Lilly Ghahremani, she believed in this work from my initial pitch. Thank you, Lilly, you are every author's dream agent!

I am also so excited to collaborate with Alex Asfour—your art is incredibly vibrant and beautiful, and I cannot imagine a better illustrator for this book. I am also so grateful to Brian LaRossa for being so open to collaborating on ideas and designs for this project.

The idea for this project was completely inspired by my three children, Jagan, Madhavi, and Arjun, who love to build, design, draw, create, explore, and investigate the world around them. When Jagan was nine years old, he said his dream was to visit the Burj Khalifa and he would ask SO many questions—"How tall is it?" "How much did it cost to make?" "Who drew the design?" Those questions and many more formed the idea for AMAZING LANDMARKS, and I am so grateful for my children's endless curiosity. I love you three the most. And please, never stop asking questions!

To my husband, Bharat, I love you. Thank you for reading each chapter draft and giving feedback even when you were overwhelmed with your own research. To my parents—my dad, who has supported every creative endeavor that I have pursued, and my mom, who inspired me to become a better reader and writer—thank you both.

This book is also for my late grandfather, K.R. Rajagopalan, who encouraged me to follow my dreams and who was never without a book in his hand. Tha-tha, I miss you every day.

—RSR